LONDON MIDLAND STEAM over Shap

LONDON MIDLAND
STEAM OVER SHAP

DEREK CROSS

D. BRADFORD BARTON LIMITED

Frontispiece: The last of her class, Patriot 4-6-0 No. 45551 miscalculates her tender capacity on Dillicar troughs, south of Tebay, on a June evening in 1962 while hurrying southwards with the 4.35 pm Carlisle-Maiden Lane perishable goods.

© copyright *D. Bradford Barton Ltd 1973*

Printed and bound in Great Britain by R.J. Acford, Chichester, Sussex

for the publishers

D. BRADFORD BARTON LTD · **Trethellan House** · **Truro** · **Cornwall**

introduction

The lonely lost call of the curlew; the harsh syncopated cackle of a north-bound 'Patriot' being thrashed; the eerie bleatings of mountain sheep in a dawn mist; that was the essence of the Lancaster & Carlisle Railway's great main line over Shap from Lancashire to the North. This was the first trunk line over the mountains in the history of railways and, though they may have been small mountains by international standards, this was very early in the steam locomotive saga and only a brave man would have attempted it. Not for nothing was it to become a railway 'Mecca' for generations of railway enthusiasts. Least of all not for nothing did the sharp and clipped name of Shap summon up visions of a hard and bitter place. Higher summits in Britain were of the future; Mitchell's conquest of Drummochter and Sharland's of Ais Gill, even the main line over Beattock, were all higher; but Shap was the first and as such has retained its own special mystique to the present day of diesels, with electrics now only a few months away.

In historical retrospect, Shap was no better than a compromise and a rather bad compromise at that. Various people had equally various ideas on how to link Lancashire and the south, with Carlisle and the north; lines round the Cumberland coast by way of Barrow and Whitehaven; or a line—which would have been the best of all—through Kendal and the Gatescarth Pass, but Kendal would have nothing to do with this. There was another scheme to follow the ambling valley of the River Lune from Lancaster and then bore a tunnel under Orton Scar and follow the tortuous valley of the Eden down to Carlisle, as the Midland eventually did. The shifting sands of Morecambe Bay killed the Barrow route, until the Furness Railway conquered this some twenty years later; the worthy citizens of Kendal ended the Gatescarth Pass idea, whilst the Lune and Eden Valley lines were both to be used, but later and not for the same project. The final Lancaster & Carlisle line was a compromise and was lucky in its engineer, for Joseph Locke—that neglected genius of early railways—was a rare combination of geologist, engineer and artist. Perhaps his greatest talent was to be able to use the landforms of a district without abusing them, an art lost on most of the motorway planners of today, alas.

Shap was a triumph, but a costly one over the years. In the cold light of hindsight it was not even remarkable scenically, apart from the one short level stretch through the Lune Gorge. Certainly it crossed the westward extension of the high Pennines and linked Carlisle as the gateway to Scotland with the south but it was a line without drama—apart from a name and a place in history. There are few major earthworks and great viaducts such as Sharland was to give to the Midland on its way north two decades later. There was no tunnel worthy of the name and with the exception of Oxenholme and Penrith no town of any importance lay on its route. Even Oxenholme was only there as Kendal in the first instance withheld its support for the railway, an aberration that they regret to this day.

Locke's great main line over this western outcrop of the Pennines falls into five parts geologically. The first is an amble along the level shore between Lancaster and Carnforth, with Morecambe Bay full of mud and mists skirting its western flank. Then a few miles of undulating pastoral country up to Oxenholme, and finally the hills onwards to Carlisle. The actual climb to Shap Summit falls into two main parts. The first hard climb, known as Grayrigg Bank, starts immediately north of Oxenholme station and rises for 6½ miles at gradients between 1 in 104 and 1 in 131 to a summit at Grayrigg station. This is followed, somewhat surprisingly, by five miles of a level or gently descending nature to the crossing of the River Lune immediately south of Tebay station. It is this central section of the old Lancaster and Carlisle that provides the most beautiful scenery of the whole line, with the rounded limestone hills of the North Pennines to the east and the harsher, more angular granites of the Lakeland mountains to the west. It also boasts rather over a mile of straight and level track known to generations of Tebay drivers as 'The Fair Mile'. Once over the Lune the upward climb begins again in earnest, with a mile and a half at 1 in 146 through Tebay station to the Greenholme I.B. signals, immediately followed by four miles at an unrelenting 1 in 75 up to Shap Summit. This four miles, for long the terror of north-bound drivers and firemen, is the notorious Shap Bank. Once over the Summit, at 916ft above sea level, the line drops steadily for 29 miles to Carlisle, the hardest part of this for south-bound trains being six miles at 1 in 125 between Eden Valley Junction and Harrison's Limeworks. This long descent to Carlisle is broken by only a very few short stretches of level track near Penrith. The country changes very subtly on the descent, from the exposed fells around Shap village to the lovely tree-lined hidden valley of the River Petterill that is followed for the last fifteen miles to the border city. As

might be expected on a line across high country, stations are few and widely spaced but, until the era of Beeching, there were no less than five branches on the stretch from Oxenholme to Carlisle. From south to north these were the Windermere branch, forking westwards immediately north of Oxenholme; one bearing eastwards down the Lune Valley at Low Gill; at Tebay the old North-Eastern line from Darlington trailing in from the east and the same company's line from Kirkby Stephen joining the L. & C. at Eden Valley Junction, some two miles south of Penrith. The latter was also the site of the final branch, that of the Cockermouth, Keswick and Penrith heading westwards towards the coast through some of the finest scenery in Lakeland.

Locomotive working over Shap has varied greatly over the years but until the end of steam the basic principle was that trains needing assistance from Carlisle to the south were always piloted, either to Shap Summit or through to Lancaster. With the advent of the more powerful Stanier locomotives this need for assistance in the up direction largely died out and if a train had to be piloted, then the assisting locomotive invariably worked through to Preston or Crewe. In the north-bound direction things were not as simple and here Oxenholme was the deciding factor, with all trains deemed able to reach there without assistance. In the case of freights these were banked in the rear from Oxenholme to Grayrigg and then again from Tebay to Shap Summit. Passenger and parcels trains frequently tackled Grayrigg Bank without assistance, even though this would have to be provided for the final five miles from Tebay onwards where a banking engine was placed at the rear of the train—though not coupled on even with passenger workings. On the other hand if a passenger or parcels train needed help on Grayrigg it certainly would on the final climb to Shap Summit, so a pilot engine was attached at Oxenholme and this worked right through to Shap Summit. There this assisting locomotive was detached and ran back 'light' to Oxenholme. This practice, known locally as "putting a sock on it", was the normal one, but was not invariable practice, for in rare cases expresses have been banked in the rear from Oxenholme to Grayrigg and again from Tebay to Summit.

The illustrations in this volume are confined to the 'mountain' section between Oxenholme and Carlisle and show as many facets as possible of steam working on what was, and probably still is, the most fascinating of all Britain's great main lines.

Near the end of steam, grimy Class 5 No. 44802 in Carlisle (Citadel) with train 1 M 31, the summer Saturday Dundee-Blackpool, in August 1967. The castellated wall in the background once supported an overall roof of the type so characteristic of many of the old L.N.W.R. stations. The roof had gone some years before this date and even the immortal Class 5's had only a year to run; the old order at this, the north end of Shap, was yielding place to the new.

Overleaf: On a sunny Sunday in August 1964, 'Duchess' Class No. 46241 *City of Edinburgh* waits in the centre road at Carlisle (Citadel) ready to work a special train of meat from Broughton—at that time the terminus of the truncated Symington to Peebles branch—to Maiden Lane, destined for Smithfield Market. By this date, displaced by diesels, the mighty Duchesses were being used more and more for fast goods work on the West Coast line.

Inside Citadel station; Standard Class 5 No. 73063 coasts into platform 3 with a local train from Glasgow via the Nith Valley line in August 1965 when alterations to the roof of the station were still in progress. The background is pure early Victoriana, complete with mullioned windows and with the bird-cage signal box (visible above the locomotive's funnel).

Contrasts at Carlisle: at the end of a busy Saturday in 1965, Class 5 No. 45340 backs through the centre road to Kingmoor sheds while Jubilee No. 45574 *India* waits on the adjacent road to work forward with a train over the Midland. In No. 4 platform, Britannia No. 70005 *John Milton* gets ready for the road with the afternoon Glasgow-Liverpool express.

A view of the south end of Citadel station in 1951 before the removal of the overall roof—a very formidable and solid structure, redolent of Moon and Webb; Patriot No. 45516 *The Bedford and Hertfordshire Regiment* pilots a Class 5 southwards with a train for the Midland route.

11

A Britannia darkens the skies to the west of Upperby Yard, making a great deal of fuss about a relatively light train. No. 70039 *Sir Christopher Wren* (minus nameplates) with a Glasgow-Liverpool express on 15 July 1967.

Class 8F 2-8-0 No. 48426 saunters up the valley of the River Petterill past Southwaite Box and its passing loops with a Crewe-bound freight on 30 September 1963. Note the Midland-type tender borrowed off an early Jubilee or long scrapped Compound.

The Wigan Scotsman. The ex-L.N.W.R. G2 0-8-0's were known as this over the whole of the Lancaster & Carlisle section and excellent engines they were for heavy goods traffic—so long as it was not in a hurry. In the late summer of 1951 a 'Super D', No. 49091, restarts a north-bound goods out of the Eamont loops at Penrith while a Class 5 waits for its turn on the main line.

Two of Stanier's masterpieces: Class 5 No. 45045 draws slowly out of the Eamont loops south of Penrith with a down goods whilst rebuilt Royal Scot No. 46169 *The Girl Guide* waits to back down into the station to work the annual Keswick Convention Special back to London. This is July 1962, still with a clutch of typical L.N.W.R. signals controlling the Keswick branch.

No. 46229 *Duchess of Hamilton* in the loops south of Penrith with a Crewe-Carlisle parcels while Class 5 No. 45255 overtakes on a Liverpool-Glasgow Saturday relief in July 1963. No. 46229 was the first of her class, exchanging nameplates with *Coronation* for an American tour in 1939. The name and number plates were never re-instated.

Ivatt Class 2MT No. 46513 pauses for breath on the Penrith Yard shunt as a Class 5 passes on the down main with a rake of empty limestone hoppers for Shap Quarry sidings. In the background is the old C.K. & P. engine shed and in the foreground the huts, the clutter and all the charm of a byegone age of railway working.

No. 46225 *Duchess of Gloucester* in one of Penrith's bay platforms ready to work the Saturdays-only Keswick-Crewe train on 22 August 1964. Other parts of this train from the Lake District were picked up at Oxenholme and Carnforth, but it still seemed a very mundane duty for so powerful a locomotive.

The thrice-weekly pick-up goods draws out of Penrith on a hot August morning in 1962 en route for Tebay, with the latter's Ivatt Class 4MT No. 43011 in charge. Fowler Class 4F No. 44081 relaxes in the sidings between bursts of shunting in the goods yard. This was the last year of these workings, as the shadow of Beeching's axe loomed ever closer.

A view of Eden Valley Junction, with the main Lancaster & Carlisle line sweeping in from the right, and that little-known branch up the Eden Valley from Penrith to Kirkby Stephen in the centre. This branch had been long closed but half a mile was still in use in August 1962 for coal traffic to the ex-North Eastern station at Clifton; traffic that was worked by the Penrith pilot as and when required. In July 1963 spotless 'Mickey Mouse' No. 46455 is seen returning to Penrith with one empty coal hopper. Note the three generations of signal, ranging (left to right) from N.E. slotted starter, L.M.S. standard upper quadrant and L.N.W.R. lower quadrant home.

The morning limestone train from Shap Quarry (known locally as Hardendale) to Ravenscraig steel works at Glasgow, on the first stage of its journey passing Harrison's Limeworks hauled by Clan Class 4-6-2 No. 72007 *Clan Mackintosh*. In 1964 these limestone trains were among the most interesting of all freights in the Carlisle area, being worked by anything that was available, from Duchesses to diesels.

The graceful lines of a Class 5 coasting down towards Penrith with a northbound goods blend with the graceful curves of the Clifton Viaduct; 12 July 1963.

The infant River Leith in the foreground skirts the line near Thrimby Grange as Class 5 No. 45039 storms towards Shap Summit with a southbound goods in August 1963.

Rebuilt Patriot No. 45527 *Southport* sweeps through Shap Station in the wet, in the midst of a summer storm in 1964 with a Saturday relief from Glasgow to London.

A rare bird during the last years of steam on the Lancaster & Carlisle, Fowler 'Crab' 2-6-0 No. 42788 tackles the last few yards through the cuttings to Shap Station with an up goods in July 1963.

Overleaf: Fowler 2-6-4T No. 42414 banks a northbound goods into Shap Summit as Fairburn's more modern equivalent No. 42095, with water overflowing from its tanks, drops back to Tebay ready for another spell of banking duty in May 1963. This was during the time of the Fairburn-Fowler change-over in the 2-6-4T's normally used to assist on Shap.

The locomotive that never was: English Electric's experimental gas turbine 4-6-0 GT 3 whispers past the summit board at the top of Shap bank on 5 October 1962 with a twelve total test train.

Summit under snow; on a bitterly cold February day in 1960, No. 45500 *Patriot*, the first of her class, tops the grade into Shap Summit with the afternoon Manchester-Carlisle semi-fast.

Shorn of its original streamlined casing but glorious in Caledonian blue livery, Duchess No. 46224 *Princess Alexandra* climbs the last half mile of 1 in 75 into the summit cutting on Shap with the down 'Royal Scot' in the summer of 1950. The sloping smokebox casing necessary for streamlining is obvious in this photograph; but alas, the glamorous 'Caley' blue livery is not! Seldom have the Duchesses looked better.

Rebuilt Scot No. 46154 *The Hussar* pilots 2-6-0 No. 42848 into the Summit cutting with a Crewe-Carlisle parcels in August 1958. The reversal of roles of pilot and train engine was common on Summer Saturdays when the pilot worked forward to Carlisle from Oxenholme after working an extra from Euston to Windermere.

Summer at Shap Wells; somehow the Fowler 2-6-4T's were the essence of Shap and once they were replaced the end of steam was nigh. No. 42424, a Tebay stalwart for many years, banks a northbound goods into the cutting above Shap Wells in 1962. The contrast with the weather on the page opposite is enough to chill the blood but such contrasts are the fascination of railways through the hills.

Winter at Shap Wells; Duchess No. 46245 *City of London* heads for Euston with 'The Royal Scot' near Shap Wells early in February 1960, with snow drifts crowding towards the line in the cuttings. A shorter train than usual was normal at this time to try and compensate for delays south of Crewe due to electrification work.

Jubilee No. 45655 *Keith* darkens the already stormy skies above Salterwath with a Wigan-Carlisle goods, shortly before a thunderstorm in August 1964.

Running repairs; even the magnificent track of the old L.M.S.R. needed attention from time to time. Fowler Class 4F 0-6-0 No. 43908 gives some attention to the permanent way half-way up Shap bank, near Salterwath, in July 1963.

Stanier Mogul No. 42977 heads northwards past Shap Wells with a Crewe-Carlisle goods in June 1960. These elegant but elusive moguls were never common on Shap.

'The Maiden Lane' was Carlisle's unofficially-named goods, conveying foodstuffs and perishables from Carlisle to London's markets. With a cargo of cattle trucks and other vans, No. 46233 *Duchess of Sutherland* coasts down Shap past Salterwath on an autumn evening in 1963.

Late evening at Salterwath as two Class 5's meet; No. 44944 rolls south with an empty stock train from Glasgow to Preston as sister engine No. 45494 climbs up the bank on a goods from Crewe. The date August 1964, but it all seems very long ago.

Six o'clock on a June morning in 1960, and Austerity 2-8-0 No. 90157 and 2-6-4T banker disturb the peace as they slog up the 1 in 75.

An early morning scene on 13 July 1963, as the doyen of the Britannia class, No. 70000, scatters steam about Scout Green with a Troop Special from Lavington to Carlisle.

Fowler 2-6-4T No. 42379 was loaned to Tebay shed for the summer of 1961 to work through trains from the north-east to Blackpool by way of the Stainmore line. She pauses here at Scout Green Box with an engineers' special. The chimney on the signal box was leaning to the last, but box, signals and Fowlers have all gone now, although the trees remain—among the very few between Tebay and Shap Summit.

Jubilee No. 45703 *Thunderer* makes the welkin ring past Scout Green Box in September 1963 with train 1S47, the morning relief to the then diesel-hauled express from Manchester and Liverpool to Glasgow. On the days when the relief ran, this was normally a Jubilee duty and some of their finest work on Shap must have been done with these trains in the dying days of steam.

Rebuilt Scot No. 46114 *Coldstream Guardsman* makes a leisurely attack on the bottom of Shap on a hot July afternoon in 1963, as it passes under the Greenholme Bridge with a London-Glasgow relief to 'The Royal Scot'.

Overleaf: Train 3L09, the morning Crewe-Carlisle parcels tackles the lower part of Shap bank with No. 46248 *City of Leeds* in charge, banked in the rear by a Fairburn 2-6-4T. By the summer of 1964, though still well maintained, Duchesses were being used more and more on mundane turns such as these.

Class 5 No. 45093 storms the lower slopes of Shap near Greenholme Bridge with a Heysham-Glasgow oil train on a bitterly cold and windy April day in 1965. The banker was one of the inevitable Fairburn 2-6-4 tanks that were in charge at Tebay at this time.

On 30 July 1960 Standard 2-6-0 No. 77002 pilots Ivatt Mogul No. 43031 into Tebay 'through the back door' with a Newcastle-Blackpool Saturday train. This summer Saturday service still survives, although running via Carlisle now that the line across the Pennines and over Stainmore has been closed and lifted. This latter was a fascinating line with its massive viaducts and ferocious grades.

'The Lakes Express' was one of the L.M.S.R.'s more evocative train names, hinting at the high Fells and deep waters of the beautiful Lake District. One of Tebay's well-kept Fowler 2-6-4 tanks No. 42359 passes through Tebay station with the five-coach Keswick portion of the up 'Lakes' on 13 July 1963. In the background Fairburn tanks wait for work up the hill.

An early Monday morning scene at Tebay with three Fowler 2-6-4 tanks preparing for work while Ivatt Class 4MT No. 43011 blows up for the pick-up goods to Penrith. One of the small Ivatt Moguls, No. 46422, gets ready for the thrice-weekly goods down the Lune Valley to Sedbergh and the improbably named Clapham Junction on the little North Western line from Lancaster to Hellifield.

The morning Crewe to Carlisle parcels charges Shap Bank past the loops at Tebay No. 2 Box in 1961 with Class 5 No. 45025 piloting No. 46224 *Princess Alexandria*. This heavy and tightly timed train was one of the very few turns that occasionally produced a piloted Duchess.

No. 46256 *Sir William Stanier* crosses the River Lune south of Tebay on 17 September 1964 with the 4.35 p.m. Kingmoor Yard (Carlisle)—Maiden Lane (London) perishable goods. This magnificent locomotive had only two weeks more service left when this photograph was taken.'The Maiden Lane', as this train was known in the far North West, was one of their last regular duties.

The fireman winds the water scoop back after filling No. 72002 *Clan Campbell*'s tender on Dillicar troughs while working a Glasgow-Manchester express on 29 June 1960. The River Lune, from which Dillicar troughs drew their water, is hidden in the deep gully behind the train.

On a dull damp day in the early summer of 1960, Patriot No. 45503 *The Leicestershire Regiment* refills its tender on Dillicar water troughs just south of Tebay heading a Territorial Army special from Newcastle to summer camp at Millom.

49

Three faces of the Lune valley: of all the lines built by Joseph Locke, that neglected genius of early railways, the three miles from Low Gill to Tebay through the Lune valley were undoubtedly his greatest. Nowhere in Britain or any other country have the hands of the artist and the engineer so brilliantly blended . . . the engineers of the M6 motorway did not have far to look for a mentor and have done every bit as well with their new road. *Opposite:* Class 5 No. 45181 works leisurely northwards with a down goods, followed a short time later by rebuilt Scot No. 46118 *Royal Welsh Fusilier* with the penultimate steam-hauled Keswick Convention Special in 1964. *Above:* One of the Princess Royal Class at speed with the morning Birmingham to Glasgow express in June 1962.

Late evening sun illuminates the side of Jubilee No. 45627 *Sierra Leone* as it heads south with an afternoon Liverpool express from Glasgow, into the Lune valley skirting the gaunt flanks of Jeffrey's Mount. At this date the shadows were as much on the future of the elegant Jubilees as they were on Locke's well designed permanent way.

Another of Stanier's elegant Jubilees, No. 45601 *British Guiana*, coasts northwards through the Lune valley with a Manchester-Glasgow express on July 1963.

Austerity 2-8-0 No. 90157 helps dig its own grave as it hustles a train of road stone through the Lune valley in July 1961. This stone, from Sandside Quarry near Arnside was for ballasting the marshalling yard at Kingmoor (Carlisle)—a new yard that meant new forms of freight working and consequently far fewer engines.

No. 46238 *City of Carlisle* heads for home and a week-end's rest on a late Saturday afternoon in July 1963 as she emerges from the north end of the Lune valley with the Saturday relief to 'The Midday Scot' from London to Glasgow.

Overleaf: A handful of cloud on a summer's afternoon darkens the eastern hills of the Lune gorge as Class 5XP No. 45571 *South Africa* hurries northwards with the Saturdays-only Blackpool-Dundee train.

Tebay's Ivatt Class 4MT No. 43028 wakes the morning echoes at Salterwath as it storms
the bank with the Sandside-Kingmoor stone train in August 1960 when this train ran daily
in connection with the construction of Kingmoor marshalling yards. The use of an Ivatt
on this train was unusual and indicated that one of the Austerity 2-8-0's allocated to Tebay
for these duties was out of service.

Class 5 No. 45081 paired to the L.M.S. self-weighing tender crosses the graceful sandstone viaduct into Low Gill with the empty stock of the last School special run for Sedbergh School on 17 September 1964. This was the end of an era, and also the end of that charming branch from Low Gill down the Lune valley to Ingleton and the 'other' Clapham Junction.

No. 46457, one of Ivatt's Class 2 Moguls, popularly known as a 'Mickey Mouse', bustles with self importance as it storms through the decaying remains of Grayrigg station in August 1960 with the District Engineers' saloon on a tour from Preston to all points north. These lively and likeable little Moguls had a near monopoly of Inspection Saloon traffic over the old Lancaster & Carlisle line in the early 1960's.

The finest permanent way in the world; this was a bold boast by the old L.N.W.R. but on the whole was justified. Yet even the finest permanent way needs to be looked after. On a sultry August afternoon in 1965, Class 8F's Nos. 48262 and 48222 head trains serving p.w. gangs carrying out repairs to the track between Lambrigg and Mosedale Hall.

A daunting load for No. 46242 *City of Glasgow* as she faces the Fells on the curve above Hay Fell with the morning Crewe-Carlisle parcels—a load that would tax any locomotive less capable than one of Stanier's Duchess Class. The hills lie ahead and there is sunshine in the air on this August day in 1963. This is what the Duchesses were designed for, the hauling of heavy trains over the great hills of northern England and southern Scotland.

Jubilee rejuvenated; No. 45695 *Minotaur*, spick and span after a spell in Crewe works, tackles the lower reaches of Grayrigg Bank with the Keswick portion of the down 'Lakes Express' on 12 July 1963. The Lakes was a favourite 'running in turn' for Crewe works; shortly after this No. 45695 came to a muddy and untimely halt in a ditch near Warrington, after being derailed.

The dying glimmer of a sunny day in October 1961 reflects on a Liverpool-bound express hauled by Rebuilt Scot No. 46124 *London Scottish*, passing under the Sedbergh road above Kendal. Approaching is Pacific No. 46228 *Duchess of Rutland* on the down 'Midday Scot'.

Evening shadows lengthen across the cutting on to Patriot No. 45547 as it coasts southward down Grayrigg Bank in October 1961 with a train of steel pipes from Mossend Yard (Glasgow). All of this class had vanished to the breakers' yards by the end of the year.

The summer Saturday Newcastle-Blackpool train appeared to strain Newcastle's carriage resources to the limit and as late as 1964 often boasted some of the older Gresley coaches in its make-up. On 27 July 1963 Class 5 No. 44709 speeds through Oxenholme with some choice vintage vehicles in its make-up whilst Class 4F No. 44440 waits for the road with the branch goods from Windermere.

Jubilee No. 45709 *Implacable* pauses at Oxenholme with a heavy Glasgow-Manchester and Liverpool express towards the end of August 1960. Class 5 No. 45464 lurks in the shadows after doing some desultory shunting with an up parcels train.

Contrasts at the north end of Oxenholme station. An extra train from Southport to Glasgow at the finish of the Glasgow Fair holiday takes a run at Grayrigg behind No. 45671 *Prince Rupert* while the same morning rebuilt Patriot No. 45523 *Bangor* eases the Windermere portion of the up 'Lake Express' off the branch and into the loop platform. Later in the day Fairburn 2-6-4T No. 42147 (above) with an afternoon train to Preston waits on the Windermere branch for one of the Fowler Class 4 tanks to vacate the station with an Oxenholme-Windermere local.

'Put a sock on it' was the curious term used amongst railwaymen when a train was assisted from Oxenholme to Shap Summit, a practice resorted to when it was likely that a passenger or parcels train had to be helped up both Grayrigg and Shap banks. On 30 July 1965 one of the early Stanier two-cylinder 2-6-4 Tanks No. 42439 and 5XP No. 45698 *Mars* restart an express from Manchester to Glasgow northwards out of Oxenholme.

Having opposed the Lancaster & Carlisle line vehemently for several years, Kendal relented too late and had to be content with a station on the Windermere branch. At the end of August 1963 Stanier two-cylinder 2-6-4T No. 42613 eases four coaches of a train from Windermere to the south past the outskirts of Kendal heading for Oxenholme.

Overleaf: The M6 now scars the flanks of Whinfell close by the location of this illustration but on a July afternoon of sunshine and showers in 1963 any motorway through the Fells was in the future and the quiet of the Lune valley was disturbed only by the ordered syncopation of Rebuilt Royal Scot No. 46165 *The Ranger* (*12th London Regiment*) as it hastened southwards with a fourteen-coach relief train from Glasgow to Euston.

There is more than a hint of frost in the air as the trail of smoke from No. 46245 *City of London* follows the contours of the hills between Grayrigg and Low Gill as this, one of the best of Stanier's Pacifics, speeds the afternoon 'Caledonian' northwards in September 1960.

The classic Class 5: No. 45481 works her way through the Lune Gorge, beneath the outline of the rounded limestone mass of Fell Head with train 1N79 the Summer Saturday Blackpool-Newcastle in July 1963. By this date, with the closing of the line over Stainmore, the train was running via Carlisle, a route no doubt more efficient but not half so interesting.

A Class 5 heading northwards with a train of military vehicles *en route* to Ayr in July 1963. Ten years ago this was the best way of mass movement of vehicles up the Lune valley but the M6 which now runs past here has altered this.

One of the last of the Oxenholme Fowler 2-6-4 tanks, No. 42378, returns homewards through the Lune valley after assisting an ailing Class 5 with a parcels train up to Shap Summit. This was one of the 2-6-4T's equipped with water scoops for long distance working as shown by the 'breather' above the tankside.

Immaculate in B.R. red livery and reeking of new paint, No. 46254 *City of Stoke-on-Trent* pauses north of Tebay for the banker with a Birmingham-Glasgow express in September 1962. The previous day she had worked the Royal Train from Balmoral over part of its journey to London.

Another of the Duchesses, No. 46236 *City of Bradford*, races southwards with the Glasgow-London 'Caledonian' over the frozen troughs at Dillicar on a bitter winter's day in February 1960.

No. 46140 *The Kings Royal Rifle Corps* waiting in the loop at the south end of Tebay Station on 18 July 1965 with the Permanent Way Dept crane returning to Carlisle. She was then one of the last two survivors of the famous Royal Scot Class.

Ivatt 4MT No. 43009 from Tebay shed clatters beneath the Greenholme road bridge towards the foot of Shap bank with the Penrith-Tebay pick-up goods on a Saturday in July 1963. For the light traffic it carried towards the end of its career—in this case three empty stone hoppers from Shap Summit—this train must have been a menace to the operating authorities who had to find a path suitable for its dilatory ways in the middle of the lunchtime procession of southbound expresses.

By some freak of nature, the main line over Shap was rarely blocked by snow for all its height. However in 1960 nature had a good try and on a day in February No. 46232 *Duchess of Montrose* tackles the last mile to the summit past Shap Wells with the Crewe-Perth semi-fast amid a very wintry landscape.

Ivatt 2-6-0 No. 43017, on loan to Tebay, puts in some useful work on a Sunday morning with a ballast train on the L. & C. main line in August 1965 at Low Gill.

A sprinkling of snow still sugars the hills about Langdale Fell on Good Friday 1951 as Patriot No. 45551 tackles Shap near Salterwath Farm with a heavy fitted freight, assisted in the rear by the inevitable Fowler Class 4P tank.

The banker drops off a northbound train of empty car-flats at Shap Summit on 31 July 1965, the train engine being a Class 9F 2-10-0. Prominent above the middle of the train is the gaunt L.N.W.R. signal box, now demolished with the onset of electrification . . . signal boxes and bankers have nothing to do with a modern railway.

With the withdrawal of the Stanier Pacifics at the end of 1964, the morning Crewe-Carlisle parcels fell heir to more humble motive power and double heading right through from Oxenholme to Shap Summit became commonplace. On an April day in 1965 with more than a hint of rain in the air 2-6-4T No. 42210 assists Class 5 No. 45200 past Shap Wells on this turn.

85

The Saturday relief to the down 'Midday Scot' passing under the Tebay road just south of Shap Quarry sidings on 31 July 1965, rather surprisingly double-headed by two Britannia Pacifics, No. 70013 *Oliver Cromwell* acting as pilot to No. 70038 *Robin Hood*.

'The Hardendale' was the bane of Kingmoor Shed's life towards the end of steam and the motive power used on it varied widely. Basically it conveyed limestone from Shap Quarry (Hardendale) to Ravenscraig steelworks south of Glasgow and Kingmoor had to supply power to work it on the first leg of its journey and anything that could turn a wheel was liable to be used. In August 1964 ex-Crosti boilered Class 9F No. 92022 passes the Quarry sidings while No. 72007 *Clan Mackintosh* prepares to propel a rake of empties to the storage hoppers. *Below:* No. 72007 makes final preparations before leaving for the north.

No. 42959, one of Stanier's secretive little moguls, with cylinder cocks open, storms through Shap station with a southbound goods on an August morning in 1964. The crane, the perfect Hornby 'O' gauge water tank and the wooden cattle pens are reminiscent of a railway era that we will not see again.

Penrith was busy on Saturdays in summer and 21 July 1962 was no exception. In the loop, Rebuilt Patriot No. 45540 *Sir Robert Turnbull* waits for the road to Carlisle with the morning goods from Harrisons Limeworks, attached in front being the Penrith pilot Ivatt mogul No. 46455 heading back to Upperby sheds at Carlisle. On the down main, No 46134 *The Cheshire Regiment* heads southward with a Glasgow-Blackpool train and on the extreme left a DMU from Keswick seeks peace in one of Penrith's bay platforms.

The annual Convention at Keswick produced the heaviest train of the year for the branch. 1967 was the last year that it was steam hauled from Penrith when it had Ivatt Class 4 moguls in charge. Here the down train heads west out of Penruddock behind Nos. 43121 and 43120. Inspector Tom Milligan, from Carlisle, exchanges rude remarks with the photographer.

On 31 August 1963, the through Keswick portion of the famous 'Lakes Express' ran for the last time. No. 46245 *City of London* had worked it into Penrith: then Ivatt mogul No. 46432, with the maximum permitted load of six coaches, had to tackle the ferocious initial grade out on to the Keswick branch at the south end of Penrith yard.

A train of long welded rails passes Penrith No. 1 Box in July 1964 hauled by Class 8F 2-8-0 No. 48750. The L.N.W.R. lower quadrant signals on the Keswick branch were to go some days later.

The infant River Petterill runs immediately beside the main line between Penrith and Plumpton where Britannia Pacific No. 70044 *Earl Haig* steams northwards with a relief to the down 'Midday Scot' in 1965.

The morning Crewe-Carlisle parcels has figured in these pages several times before and appears here for the last time coasting down into Carlisle Citadel Station behind Britannia No. 70048—with nameplates removed—in April 1965. This photograph was taken from the signalbox at the south end of the station; the Maryport & Carlisle line is to the right and the Midland route to Settle drops down on the far side of the locomotive.

With the end of steam near, the roads at Upperby Sheds at Carlisle choked with locomotives ready for the breakers' torch. Ivatts, 8F's, Black 5's and Standard Class 4's lie scattered about waiting for the kiss of death, April 1967.

in this series

GREAT WESTERN STEAM IN WALES AND THE BORDER COUNTIES

GREAT WESTERN STEAM IN DEVON — MORE GREAT WESTERN STEAM IN DEVON

GREAT WESTERN STEAM IN SOUTH WALES — GREAT WESTERN STEAM IN THE MIDLANDS

GREAT WESTERN STEAM SOUTH OF THE SEVERN — GREAT WESTERN STEAM IN CLOSE-UP

GREAT WESTERN STEAM IN CORNWALL — MORE GREAT WESTERN STEAM IN CORNWALL

BRITISH NARROW GAUGE STEAM — NE STEAM IN NORTHUMBRIA

SOUTHERN STEAM IN THE WEST COUNTRY

SOUTHERN STEAM · SOUTH AND EAST — SOUTHERN STEAM · SOUTH AND WEST

LONDON MIDLAND STEAM IN THE PEAK DISTRICT

LONDON MIDLAND STEAM OVER SHAP — LONDON MIDLAND STEAM IN THE NORTH-WEST

LONDON MIDLAND STEAM IN ACTION — LONDON MIDLAND STEAM NORTH OF THE BORDER

DIESELS ON CORNWALL'S MAIN LINE — MINERAL RAILWAYS OF THE WEST COUNTRY

CORNWALL'S RAILWAYS: A PICTORIAL SURVEY — STEAM IN THE ANDES

D. BRADFORD BARTON LTD · PUBLISHERS · TRURO